ROCKET TO EUROSTAR

The National Railway Museum in Camera

TRANSPORT

Atlantic
PUBLISHERS

Published by Atlantic Transport Publishers
Trevithick House, West End, Penryn, Cornwall TR10 8HE

Produced in association with the National Railway Museum

The Friends of the National Railway Museum Enterprises Ltd
commissioned this publication on behalf of the
Friends of the National Railway Museum

Profits from the sale of this publication support the work of
the National Railway Museum

ISBN: 0 906899 70 2

First published 1996

© Text, Friends of the National Railway Museum 1996

© Photographs (except where otherwise credited),
National Railway Museum 1996

Design and Layout: Barry C. Lane, Sutton-in-Craven

Reproduction and printing by The Amadeus Press Ltd,
Huddersfield, West Yorkshire

British Cataloguing in Publication Data.
A catalogue record for this book is available
from the British Library

ROCKET TO EUROSTAR

The National Railway Museum in Camera

Compiled and Edited
by
John Coiley
on behalf of
The Friends of the National Railway Museum

National Railway Museum York

1 LMS 4-6-2 No. 46229
Duchess of Hamilton
approaches the summit at Ais
Gill on the Settle-Carlisle line,
with a southbound 'Cumbrian
Mountain Express' in April
1982. The restoration of this
locomotive for main line
operations was the first major
project supported by the
Friends of the Museum. The
Duchess remains very much
the flagship of the Museum
and represents the great
contribution the Friends have
made, in many ways, to the
work of the Museum.

(John Hunt)

Preface

ENTHUSIASM FOR RAILWAYS has long spread wider than the engineers or entrepreneurs who created them or those who directly benefited by the travel opportunities they brought. In August 1830, George Stephenson took the young actress Fanny Kemble for a ride on the nearly completed Liverpool & Manchester Railway. Of her experience on the footplate of *Northumbrian* – a contemporary of *Rocket* – she wrote of ". . . the magical machine, with its flying white breath and rhythmical unvarying pace . . . The engine set off at its utmost speed, 35 miles an hour, swifter than a bird flies. You cannot conceive what that sensation of cutting the air was . . . I stood up, and with my bonnet off drank the air before me."

The National Railway Museum has sought from its beginnings not only to preserve the artefacts of the Railway Age but to give its visitors some flavour of the emotions they have aroused. There was early seen the need for a more formal link between the professionalism of the curatorial staff and the wider interests of many visitors. In 1977, the Friends of the National Railway Museum were founded with the twin aims of directly supporting the Museum financially and of harnessing the enthusiasm and skills of committed visitors who shared a deeply rooted love of the 'magical machines'. By March 1996 there were over 3,000 individual Friends, valued partners in many aspects of the Museum's life and work. Varied facets of that partnership, implicit and explicit, are echoed in the pages of this book.

The work of the Friends may be grouped under four broad heads. The most obvious is that of **financial support** for the Museum. Some of that support is large scale and high profile. In recent years, the Friends and the associated 229 Club have funded the maintenance and operation of the Museum's flagship locomotive, the *Duchess of Hamilton*. Finance is earmarked for a viewing gallery in the new workshop. Much else is smaller scale, but an invaluable source of ready funding when the Museum has minor but desirable needs beyond its allocated budget.

Increasingly, Friends are being used for **service in the Museum** where staff resources are inadequate within current budgets. Help with the physical restoration of exhibits, the manning of information points, the leading of gallery tours, attendance at external exhibitions and events, and assistance with the conservation of the Museum's photographic archive are current examples. Friends are meeting specific **research needs**: a group is in the later stages of producing an extensive and much needed monograph on the history of signalling.

Lastly, there are **services which enhance the value of Friend's membership** beyond Museum support and free entrance to the Museum. The quarterly Newsletter has become greatly respected, not least for its honest – even blunt – book reviews; a programme of winter lectures covers a wide variety of topics; and excursions have included both 'Eurostar' and French TGV routes.

Fanny Kemble's enthusiasm for the *Rocket* would have made her a welcome Friend. Today's Friends, in the age of 'Eurostar', help link the Museum to all whose passion for railways seeks more than a passive encounter with even the best displays. The fruits of that partnership have played a key role in much of the twenty-one years of Museum history portrayed in this book and must remain a keystone for the Museum of the future.

J. Allan Patmore
Chairman,
Friends of the National Railway Museum

2 Driving wheels from a
Bristol and Exeter Railway
broad gauge (7ft 0¼in)
locomotive of 1873 outside
the north entrance to the
National Railway Museum. A
feature of the Museum since it
opened in 1975, the wheels
with a diameter of 8ft 10in,
were the largest used in
Britain and present a railway
image for visitors and
passers-by alike.

(NRM: 67/85)

Foreword

IT WAS IN BRITAIN that the modern railway first emerged and Britain was the first country to be transformed by the economic development stimulated by the railway revolution. It is perhaps not surprising, therefore, that interest in our railway heritage has been high in Britain for many years.

With that interest has gone a passion which was well demonstrated when it was first proposed that a National Railway Museum should be set up outside London. Never before had the Nation's collections been taken to a centre away from the Capital for display. The arguments for and against were made far and wide, not least in Parliament and the letters pages of The Times.

The National Railway Museum opened on 27th September 1975, 150 years to the day after the opening of the Stockton and Darlington Railway. The decision to locate it in York was vindicated in the years that followed, which have seen more than 18 million visitors pass through its doors.

For much of the last twenty years, Dr John Coiley was Head of the Museum and in these pages, he shows us something of the wide range of activity that takes place, much of it not obvious to the public. The Museum's twin tasks of caring for the vast national collection of railway material and of helping the public to understand more about railways provide it with a vast stage on which to perform. The NRM has always been keen to loan material to other Museums, to demonstrate its vehicles and other objects on and off site and to provide a wide range of research services to its users. Whilst other museums ponder how to connect with a broader public, how to open their doors and take their collections out, the NRM has done it.

This book provides us with the opportunity to stop and draw breath after 21 years of success in York. It also provides a starting point for 21 more exciting years. Dr Coiley hints at the changes which have taken place since the Museum opened. Britain's railways have changed, as has the relationship between the public and the railways. Without change to record, there would be no need for a Museum but the Museum itself must change to ensure that it stays relevant for new generations.

The next 21 years therefore promise to be equally eventful for the National Railway Museum. They are likely to see the emphasis shift from the urgent collection of evidence of a rapidly disappearing era to the provision of access to collections for researchers and the explanation to a new generation of the real significance of the railway age.

As we approach the millenium and the two hundredth anniversary of steam locomotion, the information revolution is providing the tools which are already transforming our lives and our concept of distance. The National Railway Museum is already beginning to use the tools that this new era provides and it is they which will shape what the Museum can offer its users in the future. But the story the Museum tells – of a technology invented in north east England which changed the world – will continue to be worth telling and will continue to be told in an imaginative and exciting way to new generations of visitors here in York.

Andrew Scott
Head,
National Railway Museum

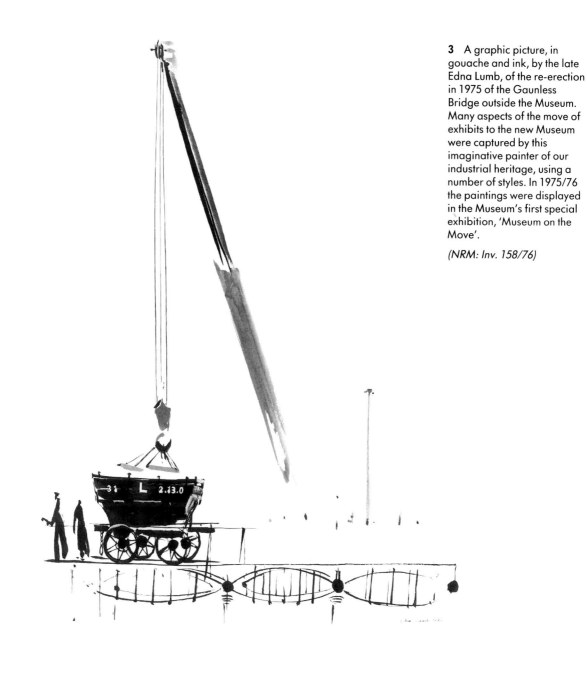

Introduction

THIS COLLECTION of photographs has been produced on the occasion of the 21st anniversary of the National Railway Museum, York, which opened in 1975. The photographs provide a private view 'behind the scenes' of the National Railway Collections, past and present. The initiative for the publication came from the Friends of the National Railway Museum.

To help appreciate this presentation a few words about the National Railway Museum — its origins, developments and plans for the future — may be appropriate. The railway as we know it today was invented in Britain at the beginning of the last century. It is perhaps a telling measure of the very great significance for society of the coming of the railway, that some of the earliest examples of steam locomotives were preserved at a time when our technical heritage, as distinct from the promotion of new achievements, was scarcely considered.

In due course the interest and value of historical railway relics began to be appreciated more widely. Some of the many private railway companies started to set aside selected historical equipment, albeit mainly locomotives. It was not until 1927 however that the newly established London and North Eastern Railway opened the first museum in Britain dedicated to railways, in Queen Street, York. This was followed, after the nationalisation of the railways in 1948, by the Museum of British Transport at Clapham, London in 1961-3. The Transport Act of 1968, however, saw responsibility for the railway relics pass from the British Railways Board to the Department of Education and Science, which meant in effect, the Science Museum at South Kensington. Since there was no room in the Science Museum for the collections then at York and Clapham, the British Railways Board was also required to provide a suitable building. After much debate, a former motive power depot in York (a leading tourist city with major railway interests) was chosen and converted to house the new National Railway Museum, the first national museum (as part of the Science Museum) out of London.

The collections displayed in the National Railway Museum when it opened in 1975 were essentially an amalgamation of those previously exhibited at York and Clapham with some important additional material. These collections ranged from famous steam locomotives, through royal saloons, complicated signalling equipment, elegant tableware, magnificent posters to mundane but fascinating tickets. The exhibitions filled the new Museum and proved very popular with visitors but much remained to be done.

First, there was a demand for material which had been in store for many years to be restored and put on exhibition. Only some of these exhibits could be accommodated at York so a number of locomotives and items of rolling stock were placed on long term loan with some of the private preserved railways which were flourishing and supported the Museum in many ways. There were also increasing expectations for the Museum to continue to provide historic working steam locomotives for special trains on the main line following the lead taken by the Railways Board in 1971 with the 'Return to Steam' programme. These and other restoration projects were greatly assisted by the founding in 1977 of the Friends of the NRM, a charitable body with the objective of supporting the work of the Museum.

Notwithstanding a lower profile but equally important, there was much work to be done 'behind the scenes'. This included sorting, listing and cataloguing the many different collections which had been taken over from the British Railways Board, as well as establishing a small reference library and associated archive. Resources had also to be devoted to running the new educational services as well as workshops and the photographic studio.

The combination of acquisitions and newly restored material, especially locomotives and rolling stock, called for more premises, initially for storage and ultimately for public display in an expanded Museum. Such growth would allow the 'balance' of the collection to be improved by including exhibits representing modern motive power, ordinary carriages, freight wagons and the private railway industry including equipment built for service overseas.

Gradually suitable buildings were acquired either adjoining the Museum or close by. In 1989, before they were all properly operational, the roof of the main Museum building was condemned as unsafe, due to the deterioration of the reinforced concrete roof beams. This meant the building would be closed to visitors and staff from April 1990. Rather than completely close the Museum it was decided to open the former goods depot, used for storage and restoration work since 1976, with a temporary exhibition, 'The Great Railway Show'. This was to be mainly about travel by train with a special interactive section for younger visitors. It would be subsequently incorporated in the expanded Museum when the failed roof had been replaced by one of a striking new design.

The new National Railway Museum opened in April 1992. In spite of the greater coverage and enhanced displays it was becoming evident that visitors and indeed the public in general were less aware of railways and railway history than previously. A new approach was obviously needed to prepare the museum for the next century.

In his foreword Andrew Scott outlines what is to be done and Professor Allan Patmore's preface explains how the Friends of the Museum can assist. When these improvements are realised they should enable the Museum to achieve its aim of helping the visitor to enjoy and understand the history and contemporary development of the railway.

John Coiley
Head, 1975-92,
National Railway Museum

4 *Puffing Billy*, built in 1813 by William Hedley, photographed in the 1860s at the end of its active life, is displayed in the Science Museum, London. It is part of the National Railway Collection and is significant as one of the two oldest steam locomotives extant. That it has been preserved at all is a measure of the great impact the railways had on a society unaccustomed to technical museums and preserving the industrial past.

(ScM: 2498/77)

5 The framework of an early wagon, c.1815, from the Belvoir Castle Tramway. The early wagons, not as spectacular or as durable as the early locomotives, were not unfortunately retained or recorded to the same extent as the motive power. Nevertheless, a few examples of these important relics of early railways survive in Britain and mainland Europe. The remains of this vehicle with flanged wheels running on fish-bellied cast iron edge rails, compared with earlier plain wheels and plateway tracks, indicated the way forward for the carriage of both goods and, later, passengers.

(NRM: CT RE 5)

6 *Rocket* on arrival at the Science Museum in 1862. Built in Newcastle in 1829 *Rocket* achieved lasting recognition by winning the Rainhill Trials later that year. During the next few years, while working on the Liverpool and Manchester Railway, *Rocket* received a number of modifications. The most notable of these was the lowering of the cylinders to improve stability at speed and the fitting of a smokebox. After ending its working life at a colliery in the north of England, *Rocket* was subsequently set aside for preservation. It received limited restoration at the Stephenson & Co works in Newcastle before being taken into the Patent Office Collection of the Science Museum in London. It is not clear exactly when or why it assumed the form shown in the photograph. It was another thirty years or so however before it was modified to its present form which is thought to represent more closely its appearance while working on the Liverpool and Manchester Railway. The problems of restoration were already emerging.

(ScM: 456/56)

7 The original *Locomotion* of 1825 and designed by George Stephenson, near Shildon, Co. Durham in 1925, at the head of a train of chaldron wagons in the Cavalcade to celebrate the 100th anniversary of the opening of the Stockton and Darlington Railway. Although this important historical locomotive appears to be hauling the train, it was powered by a petrol engine hidden in the tender.

(NRM: DAR 1158)

8 A 1930s scene in the first museum in Britain dedicated to railways, located in a former locomotive workshop, in Queen Street, York. This museum was opened in 1927 by the LNER following the celebrations in 1925 to mark the 100th anniversary of the Stockton and Darlington Railway. Having gathered together many historical railway relics, large and small, for these celebrations the newly formed LNER decided to establish a permanent display of this material, open to the public.

(NRM: 2846/12/60)

9 Great Northern Railway 4-2-2 express passenger locomotive No. 1 leaving King's Cross in 1938 with a special train of old GNR carriages of the kind used on the *Flying Scotsman* express of 1888. This train was one of a number run that summer to celebrate the 50th anniversary of the railway race to Edinburgh, when the East Coast companies competed with their West Coast rivals. This famous 1870 locomotive, with just one pair of large 8ft diameter driving wheels, had been in the Railway Museum at York since 1927 before being removed and overhauled for this anniversary. This use of an historic locomotive from a museum collection established a precedent which was to be followed many times during the next sixty years despite the costs involved and the risk of damage.

(NRM: C.C.B. Herbert Collection)

10 The collections of the Railway Museum at York became known not only for their locomotives but also for the many other artefacts, a number of which are seen here. Many of these items were familiar to passengers as a result of their travels by train and so were of interest to museum visitors.

(NRM: BR(ER) CCE 1744)

11 The Railway Museum also had a gallery devoted to small objects such as models, crests, tableware etc as well as printed papers and records. This gallery was located in the former hotel building of the early station inside the city walls. Over the years these archive collections became a place of study of railway history especially that relating to the north of England. The small exhibits gallery closed in the early 1970s; objects and material relating to relics were set aside for the new National Railway Museum and archive material transferred to the Public Record Office at Kew.

(NRM: BR(ER) CCE 62135/812 89)

12 A glimpse of the Transport Treasures exhibition in 1956 in the Shareholders' Room of the old Euston Station. After nationalisation in 1948 of the railways and much public transport it was soon realised that there was a need for a new larger museum not only for railways but encompassing the other activities of the nationalised body. The first step in this direction was the appointment, from the museum world, of a Curator for Historical Relics, the late John Scholes who was advised by a Consultative Panel with specialist transport experience. While material for the new museum was being selected, collected and restored a number of exhibitions of objects already secured were staged, some in these elegant surroundings at Euston.

(NRM: BRB 3374)

13 GWR 'Castle' Class 4-6-0 No. 4073 *Caerphilly Castle* in the streets of west London in 1961. Following cosmetic restoration at Swindon the locomotive was on its way to become a major exhibit in the new Land Transport Gallery at the Science Museum alongside *Puffing Billy*, *Rocket* and the prototype 'Deltic' diesel-electric locomotive. With the end of steam on British Railways approaching, a number of famous locomotives were made available to museums with strong regional or technical interests.

(R.C. Riley)

14   The main hall of the Museum of British Transport, Clapham, south London. The museum opened in 1961/3 and initially included, as well as much railway material, exhibits representing London Transport, trams, inland waterways and heavy goods vehicles. The main display, in a former bus garage, was typical for the period with major exhibits such as locomotives and carriages on small plinths creating a 'museum' atmosphere rather than one of railways despite the industrial nature of the building. A very high proportion of the restored objects then available were displayed, with little stored in a reserve collection in the museum.

(NRM: BRB 41/2)

15   Small and fragile objects were displayed at Clapham in cases of the kind already used for the earlier temporary exhibitions.

(NRM: BRB 11024)

16 Although the regular use of steam on British Railways ended in 1968, steam was approved for main line charter trains in 1971 a decision celebrated with a 'Return to Steam' special hauled by GWR 4-6-0 No. 6000 *King George V'*. This locomotive, part of the National Collection, was made available through the co-operation of the British Railways Board with the custodians (the GWR Museum, Swindon), the sponsors (Bulmers Ltd, Hereford) and the operating team of volunteers (the 6000 Locomotive Association). This was an early example of the good collaboration and enthusiasm required to enable the operation of special trains on the main line using historic steam locomotives. *King George V* continued in demand for special trains and is seen here in later years working between Shrewsbury and Hereford.

(John Hunt)

17 Locomotives in store in the former works of the Pullman Car Company at Preston Park, Brighton. Interesting historic material continued to become available throughout the 1960s as a result of the 1955 Modernisation Plan and the long overdue general overhaul of the railway system. Locomotives, carriages, wagons and signal equipment, selected by the Curator of the Museum of British Transport with the advice of the Consultative Panel, were stored under cover at a number of rail connected locations, culminating in Preston Park.

(ScM: 1698/74/06)

18 An aerial view of York motive power depot, which was to become the National Railway Museum, in the late 1950s. The depot is being rebuilt to accommodate diesel-electric locomotives in a new straight road shed alongside the East Coast Main Line. At the same time the roof over the two remaining turntables is also rebuilt, replacing the temporary repairs following the bomb damage in 1942.

(NRM: Neg. 430/2)

19   A closer view of the rebuilding of the motive power depot roof over the retained turntables (two out of the original four). The new support girders can be clearly seen together with the curved reinforced concrete transverse beams. It was these latter beams which failed in the late 1980s.

(NRM: BR (ER) CCE 6293)

20   A typical view in the steam locomotive side of the rebuilt motive power depot, York, towards the end of active steam in the depot in 1966. The turntable in the foreground was renewed in 1954 and is still in regular use by the Museum.

(John Hunt)

21 Work in progress in October 1973 to convert the York motive power depot for use as the new National Railway Museum. The traditional floor consisting of 'sets' has been dug up and will be replaced by a smooth synthetic material. The structural girders and transverse reinforced concrete beams, dating from the late 1950s, are retained but the roof fabric will be renewed with more modern materials, with translucent sections.

(ScM: 1248/73/09)

22 Autumn 1974 and the 1840 Stockton and Darlington Railway carriage is moved out of the old Railway Museum, for transfer on a railway wagon to the new National Railway Museum. The all wooden vehicle was the first to be transferred and required special care. First it was wheeled on to a special length of track and then track and carriage were lifted together so that the carriage structure was not strained. The steam crane had been sent from Leeds and was typical of the care taken by British Railways, overall and locally, with the transfer of their collections to the new Museum.

(NRM CT RE 22)

23 Removal of locomotives from the Queen Street Museum had always been difficult. Awkward slewing of track inside the building was a precursor to operations. Outside a support had to be built for the exit siding where it crossed the edge of a small turntable pit. The limited head shunt meant that the final positioning of each locomotive called for manual effort – 'pinch' bars behind wheels and shoulders to buffers and other even less conventional methods.

(NRM: RE 23)

24   A special train was arranged to take most of the exhibits, other than locomotives and carriages, from the Clapham rail head at Stewart's Lane to York. The train is seen here in north London and contains a number of special wagons for loads such as the broad gauge wheels. It also included a carriage for the British Transport Police who accompanied the valuable collections.

(ScM: 2030/74/07)

25   The special train of exhibits also included a number of old road/rail containers on flat wagons which were filled with many hundreds of small objects and records. These could be positioned within the rail connected new Museum and unloaded undercover with security and when required.

(ScM: 779/75/02)

26 Some of the smaller locomotives were moved north from London on 'Weltrol' and similar wagons. A number of such loads are seen here being unloaded immediately outside the Museum in the area that subsequently became the public car park.

(NRM: CT 75/07/20)

27 One of the more unusual standard gauge locomotives in the National Collection is the diminutive Shropshire and Montgomeryshire Railway 0-4-2WT *Gazelle* built in 1893. It is seen here being returned by the Army, with due ceremony, after a long term loan to the Longmoor Military Railway in Hampshire. It is now on loan to the Museum of Army Transport in Beverley, East Yorkshire.

(NRM: Y/095/65/12)

28 Although the new National Railway Museum was due to open on 27th September 1975, the exact 150th anniversary of the opening of the Stockton and Darlington Railway, the main celebrations, including a Cavalcade as in 1925, were planned for the holiday month of August. The NRM provided a number of historic locomotives for the occasion, including several in steam. Some of these had taken part in the 1925 event including NER 2-4-0 No. 910. This locomotive is seen here at night in the yard outside the Shildon Wagon Works. In 1975 No. 910 was not in steam however and was hauled in the Cavalcade by privately owned LNER A3 class 4-6-2 No. 4472 *Flying Scotsman*.

(John Hunt)

29 While the arrangements at Shildon went very smoothly overall, there were minor mishaps. Here the Museum's BR standard Class 9 2-10-0 No. 92220 *Evening Star*, the last steam locomotive built for British Railways in March 1960 at Swindon, has a problem with the sidings at Shildon. Fortunately blocks of wood and a good pull from a diesel shunter soon had all the wheels back on the rails.

(NRM: CT 75/19/23)

30 After the Cavalcade at Shildon the Museum locomotives returned to York and were pictured outside the Museum in the late evening. Midland Railway compound 4-4-0 No. 1000, which had hauled veteran NER 2-4-0 No. 910 back south, is disposing of its fire while *Evening Star* awaits its turn on the ash pit.

(J.C. Beckett)

31 While the Stockton and Darlington celebrations were taking place preparations for opening the Museum continued apace at York. After cleaning exhibits were covered with dust sheets to keep the need for further attention to a minimum. A shortage of the normal linen sheets led to the use of spare plastic wrapping and this unusual appearance for LNWR 2-2-2 No. 1868 *Columbine* of 1845.

(J.C. Beckett)

32 During September 1975 exhibits continued to arrive for inclusion in the new Museum. For large exhibits reaching York by road, low bridges near the Museum meant alternative arrangements were necessary for the final access. From the outset the then BREL Carriage Works were always most helpful and their sidings were used to unload NER Bo-Bo 'Steeple Cab' electric locomotive No. 1 on its arrival from storage at the Industrial Museum, Leicester. After unloading and checking, the locomotive was hauled the short distance to the NRM, via the East Coast Main Line, by a yard pilot.

(NRM: CT 75/24/35)

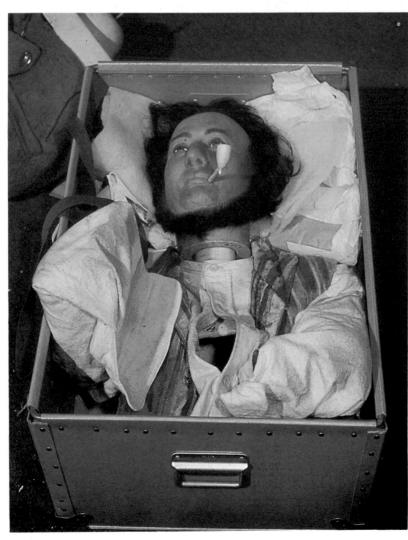

33 There also remained many boxes to unpack, some with surprising contents.

(NRM: CT RE 33)

34 There was not room in the new Museum Main Hall for all the locomotives previously on display in York and Clapham, together with newly acquired locomotives and carriages. The opening of a new museum, devoted to the Stockton and Darlington Railway, at North Road Station, Darlington to mark the 150th anniversary of the railway, enabled SDR (NER) 'long boiler' 0-6-0 No. 1275 to be displayed there on a long term loan together with NER 2-4-0 No. 1463.

(NRM: CT 75/22/02)

35 His Royal Highness, the Duke of Edinburgh, opens the National Railway Museum on 27th September 1975.

(NRM: RE 35)

36 Of the new displays perhaps the one which attracted the most interest was the sectioned steam locomotive. The locomotive chosen for this treatment was the rebuilt former Southern Railway 'Merchant Navy' class 4-6-2 No. 35029 *Ellerman Lines*. As well as sectioning both locomotive and tender, the driving wheels were made to rotate, by means of an electric friction drive, so that visitors could watch valve gear events in slow motion in one of the outside cylinders. Unlike earlier sectioned locomotives the sectioning was selective so retaining in part the full width of smoke-box, boiler and fire-box to assist the understanding of the construction and operation.

(NRM: CT RE 36)

37 Another new feature in the NRM was the deepening of one of the original depot inspection pits to enable visitors to walk underneath a locomotive with ease and in safety. Such an arrangement allowed an examination of components such as cylinders, valve gear and firebox/ashpan very often hidden between the wheels and frames. This facility is especially helpful when studying British locomotives many of which have two inside cylinders. This is in marked contrast in general, to European and North American practice where most of the vital operational components could be seen from alongside the locomotive.

(NRM: CT RE 37)

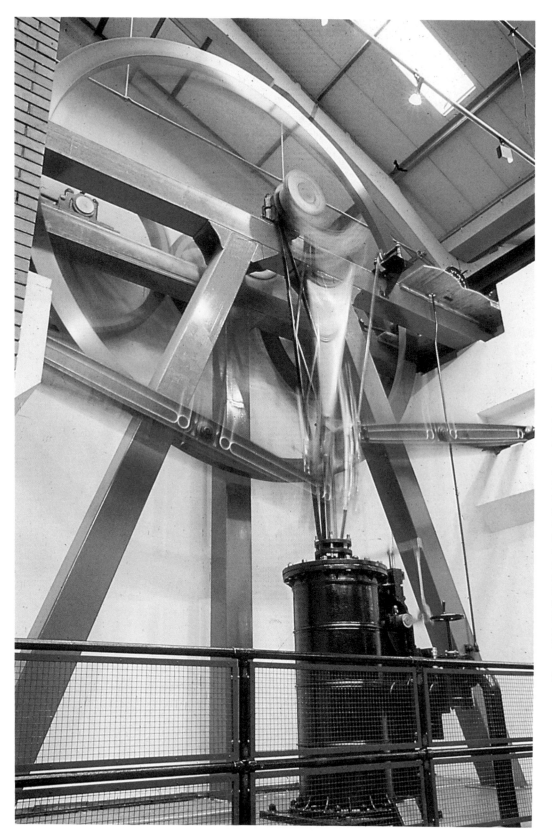

38 The Weatherhill Winding Engine of 1833 from Stanhope in Co. Durham was another exhibit to attract much attention. When it went into the old Railway Museum it had been necessary to cut the original large fly wheel in half due to limited headroom. In keeping with Science Museum traditions it was decided that it should be capable of demonstration when transferred to the NRM. The flywheel was replaced and the engine driven by electric friction drive onto the rim of the flywheel. While this is eyecatching when demonstrated, it is not easy to understand the original function of the engine without the cable winding drum. Perhaps one day a small scale model/diorama will assist in this respect . . .?

(NRM: CT RE 38)

39 The Museum was provided with well equipped precision workshops from the opening. This was a change from the museums at York and Clapham when any such work would have been carried out in one of the many long established railway workshops. Equipment and facilities in the NRM were gradually expanded to meet the demands of maintaining steam locomotives and carriages in operating condition. It was however to be some 10 years before anything approaching proper maintenance and restoration workshops would be available.

(NRM: CT RE 39)

40 The initial display of permanent way equipment such as rails, chairs and sleepers, from the earliest wooden wagonways to the latest continuously welded rails was in an essentially traditional style. It relied mainly on simple labels to explain this fundamental if unglamorous aspect of railways and was difficult for most visitors to understand. It was not until the expansion of the Museum in 1992 that with more space and new displays and carefully selected videos that the general visitor has been able to appreciate the importance of the permanent way and the progress made since the first railways.

(NRM: CT RE 40)

41 The original display of signal and telegraph (S&T) equipment enjoyed a rather higher profile than that for the permanent way items. Nevertheless, despite any familiarity on the part of the visitor with the traditional semaphore signal etc, it proved difficult to explain the working of the signalling system using only original equipment, historic or modern. Demonstrations in the Museum lecture theatre where special models were available overcame some of these problems. It was not however until the displays were revised and videos introduced that there was a marked improvement in presentation for the visitor.

(NRM: CT RE 41)

42 As well as demonstrations of the larger exhibits including, on special occasions, a locomotive in steam, a number of smaller exhibits in show cases could be made to work. In some exhibits the operation simply conveyed some sense of movement, in others as here it allowed the visitor some control. In this instance valve events may be studied while the wheels are driven and the forward/reverse mechanism examined. Perhaps however the most important role for this model is simply to involve the visitor.

(NRM: CT RE 42)

43 The former NER goods depot in Leeman Road, York, opposite the motive power depot, photographed about the beginning of this century. Wagon load goods traffic declined steadily from the 1950s and by 1976 most of this building and associated yards and sidings were for sale. Still looking very much as in this photograph the premises were acquired by the Museum for urgently needed storage.

(NRM: 1188/79)

44 The interior of the Leeman Road goods depot about 1961, showing an early small fork lift truck at work. Lighting would still appear to be by gas.

(NRM: 470/85)

45 The interior of the main part of the goods depot shortly after acquisition by the Museum. The platform sidings are already filled with locomotives stored or undergoing maintenance and carriages and wagons awaiting restoration. The platforms are beginning to be covered with relics, especially S&T equipment, newly acquired from British Rail. Not all the building was available at this time for Museum use so that it was fortunate that other material could remain in the old Queen Street Museum until it was demolished in 1979.

(NRM: CT 76/48/24)

46 A view of the Museum from the cab of the gas-turbine powered Experimental Advanced Passenger Train (APT-E). This revoluntionary 4 car tilting train had just reached the Museum, under its own power, after completing extensive trials in the early 1970s. The train was an important acquisition since it illustrated the Museum's policy of explaining the railway story, past, present and future.

(NRM: 2375/76)

47 Two of the older Museum locomotives in action together. Restored to working order, primarily for the Stockton and Darlington celebrations the previous summer, LNWR 2-4-0 No. 790 *Hardwicke* pilots MR compound 4-4-0 No. 1000 away from York with a special train to Harrogate and Leeds.

(NRM: CT 76/09/25)

48 When veteran cars from all over Europe visited the Museum it was an opportunity for Museum staff testing *Evening Star* and the crew of a Stanley steam car to explore one another's machines.

(NRM: CT 76/14/31)

49 The local British Rail breakdown team come to the Museum's assistance. To transfer a narrow gauge locomotive (the first Beyer-Garratt, on loan from the Festiniog Railway) from a road low loader to a well wagon for ease of display in the Museum, specialist equipment was required. With this, comprising adjustable support pads moved by a hydraulic system, it was possible to slide the locomotive from one vehicle to the other.

(NRM: CT 76/23/12)

50 Newly restored freight wagons displayed outside the Museum. In the early years of the Museum the acquisition and restoration policies aimed at broadening the coverage of the displays, especially locomotives and rolling stock. While the attraction of the Royal Saloons and other special carriages was appreciated, typical carriages were increasingly included in exhibitions together with wagons and, in due course, examples of the first generation of modern motive power.

(NRM: CT 76/46/32)

51 The 100th anniversary of the opening in 1876 of the Midland Railway line from Settle to Carlisle was marked in the Museum by the 'Wheels in the Wilderness' special exhibition. Such occasions provide an opportunity to display material not usually seen and in this case featured a range of smaller objects associated with the Midland Railway as well as illustrative archive material reflecting the difficulties of building this railway.

(NRM: 1433/76)

52 The period interior of the NER Dynamometer car of 1906. This vehicle was included in the test train in 1938 when on 3rd July LNER A4 class 4-6-2 No. 4468 *Mallard* set a world speed record of 126mph (203kph) for steam locomotives, a record which still stands today. Although visitors are not usually admitted to carriages the extensive glazing of this vehicle allows a good view of the fascinating interior.

(NRM: 307/76)

53   On 31st May 1977 Sir
Peter Parker, then Chairman
of the British Railways Board,
opened a special exhibition
on 'Royal Railway Travel', the
Museum's contribution to the
celebrations to mark the
Silver Jubilee of Her Majesty
Queen Elizabeth II. Sir Peter
afterwards attended the
Inaugural Dinner of the
Friends of the National
Railway Museum (FNRM),
held in the Museum and
responded to the toast to the
Friends by the late Rt. Rev. Dr.
Eric Treacy, Bishop of
Wakefield.

(NRM: Print RE 53)

54   LBSCR 0-4-2 No. 214
Gladstone decorated for the
Silver Jubilee special
exhibition. This locomotive
was the first major exhibit in
the old Railway Museum in
York not to have originated
from the north-east. When
Gladstone was withdrawn by
the Southern Railway in the
1920s it was acquired by the
Stephenson Locomotive
Society who lent it to the old
Museum before donating it in
1959.

(NRM: 2607/77)

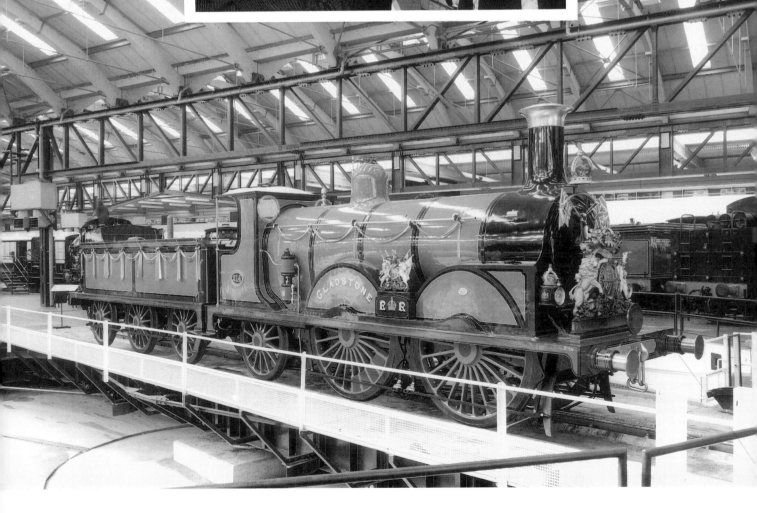

55 *Mallard* outside the Museum with another A4 class 4-6-2, the visiting privately preserved No. 4498 *Sir Nigel Gresley* named after the designer of the class and other famous LNER locomotives. The occasion was graced by the presence of Mrs Godfrey, Sir Nigel's daughter and members of her family.

(NRM: 1121/79)

56 Evidence, after bad weather, that major repairs were needed to the roof of the goods depot store.

(NRM: 052/77)

57 An evening view of the exhibition of locomotives and carriages, past and present, assembled to celebrate the 100th anniversary of York station, designed by Thomas Prosser for the North Eastern Railway.

(J.R. Carter)

58 After the Inaugural General Meeting of the Friends of the National Railway Museum on 15th October, the Museum was presented with their first donation. This was a fine Gauge I tinplate model of the GWR 'Atbara' class 4-4-0 No. 3410 *Sydney*, made in 1908 by Bing for Bassett-Lowke. Priced in the Bassett-Lowke catalogue of the time at £2.2s.0d. this well preserved model was bought for the Museum for some £400.

(NRM: 143/96)

59 The NER Q7 class 0-8-0 No. 901 (here as BR No. 63460) heads a train of unrestored locomotives being hauled north to the Museum and photographed in north London in November 1977. These locomotives had been stored in the former Pullman Car Works at Preston Park, Brighton, for a number of years and were being moved by British Rail as one of its final commitments to establishing the National Railway Museum. After only a short stay in York, No. 63460 moved on loan to the North Yorkshire Moors Railway. There it was restored to working order by the North Eastern Locomotive Preservation Group and is now in regular use on that line.

(David Eatwell)

60 A craftsman carefully removes varnish from the East Coast Joint Stock passenger brake van of 1908, in the Carriage Works at Doncaster. The vehicle had just been acquired by the Museum from the Royal Train fleet and was in excellent condition, only a few teak panels requiring replacement. Fears at this time that the skills and knowledge of these craftsmen would be lost on their retirement have not been justified.

(NRM: CT 77/19/19)

61 An Andrew Barclay fireless 0-4-0 locomotive of 1956 arrives at the Carriage Works, York, en route for the Museum. Locomotive No. 1 of the Imperial Paper Mills at Gravesend, Kent, was bought by a schoolboy who kindly donated it to the Museum to fill a gap in the collection.

(NRM: 730/78)

62 The Museum LNER 2-6-2 No. 4771 *Green Arrow* at Carlisle in March 1978 after working the first steam train over the Settle-Carlisle line since the last regular steam train on British Rail in August 1968. Emerging from beneath the locomotive is the late Bill Harvey, a former renowned shedmaster on BR. A champion of the steam locomotive, Bill Harvey will always be associated with Green Arrow in particular. He was of great help to the Museum's engineering staff over the restoration and operation of this locomotive.

(NRM: CT 78/05/21)

63 The British Rail paddle steamer *Lincoln Castle* at Hull in early 1978, after being withdrawn from the Hull-New Holland service. There was considerable interest for the Museum to acquire this vessel for display on loan in Hull. Although the BRB eventually agreed that the *Lincoln Castle* could be claimed under the terms of the 1968 Transport Act, the Museum and the local support groups could not justify the berthing fees. The vessel was sold and privately preserved first near the new Humber Bridge and then in Grimsby.

(NRM: CT 78/07/27)

64 The Canterbury and Whitstable Railway 0-4-0 locomotive *Invicta* of 1829 is refurbished in the Museum goods depot store for the Railway's 150th anniversary. When the Science Museum agreed to help the Transport Trust with this task the NRM was already fully committed. The Friends however were able to arrange help from the embryonic evening working party, comprised largely of members of the York Railway Circle.

(Dr. A.J. Lowe)

65 A corner of the 'Grand Hotels' special exhibition, to celebrate the 100th anniversary of the Royal Station Hotel, York which was devoted to the story of railway owned hotels. As with all other areas of railway operations the Museum had already received considerable assistance from the catering and hotel divisions. This exhibition was another opportunity to display some of the many fine items acquired but for which sufficient exhibition space was not normally available.

(NRM: 353/78)

66 NER P3 class 0-6-0 No. 2392 on the larger turntable in the Museum while on loan from the North Eastern Locomotive Preservation Group. This loan was a good example of the help the Museum has received from the railway preservation movement and the benefits of mutual co-operation. The Group knew the Museum was looking for an 0-6-0 locomotive, the 'workhorse' of the railways, since its own examples had already been committed on long term loans. Their locomotive although spotless required costly maintenance and they were looking for a secure undercover home for it while they raised the necessary funds.

(John Hunt)

67 Help for the Works, publicity for the Museum when GNR 'Atlantic' 4-4-2 No. 251, built at Doncaster in 1902, returns to its birthplace, along with other Doncaster built Museum locomotives, for a special Works Open Day.

(NRM: CT 78/09/14)

68 A display of East Coast Main Line motive power, covering many years, in the Scarborough platforms of York station and used during the making of a TV programme on the 'Railway Races to the North'. In addition to *Mallard* and No. 251 seen here, the Museum also provided NER 4-4-0 No. 1621, GNR 'Single' 4-2-2 No. 1 and LNWR 2-4-0 No. 790 *Hardwicke*.

(Gavin Morrison)

69 To mark the 100th anniversary of on-train catering, the Museum together with British Rail's catering arm Travellers Fare, arranged a tour of historic dining cars around Britain. At several points along the route it was possible for the public to buy special tickets to travel and dine on the train. The 'Centenary Express' is seen here passing the site of Allerton station, between Knaresborough and York, on the last leg of its tour, hauled by LNER 2-6-2 No. 4771 *Green Arrow*.

(Gavin Morrison)

70 The interior of the shell of an electric motor from a class 84 Bo-Bo 25kV electric locomotive, one of many items in a special exhibition for the 100th anniversary of the use of electric power on railways. The first practical electric railway was demonstrated by Werner von Siemens in Berlin in 1879 using a small locomotive with a 3hp motor collecting current at 150 volts from a centre third rail.

(NRM: CT RE 70)

71 Steam trials of a reproduction of the famous *Rocket* of 1829 at Springwell, Co. Durham. Following the interest aroused in 1975 by the working reproduction of George Stephenson's *Locomotion*, the Science Museum asked the late Michael Satow, who had masterminded that project to repeat the exercise and to build a working reproduction of *Rocket* for the National Railway Museum. This he did as part of a Work Training scheme and the reproduction *Rocket* was demonstrated in Kensington Gardens, London, in September 1979. This marked the 150th anniversary of the Rainhill Trials in Lancashire, when the original *Rocket* first proved its prowess.

(NRM: CT 79/09/10)

72 The former GWR Manor House Hotel, Moretonhampstead, Devon, photographed for the record by staff during a visit to discuss what hotel artefacts (such as tableware), records and photographs might be acquired by the Museum. Buildings and many engineering structures present a problem for the Museum and those interested in railway history. At best, they have to be visited on site or, if demolished, then future study is wholly dependent on what plans, records and photographs may have survived.

(NRM: CT 79/09/01)

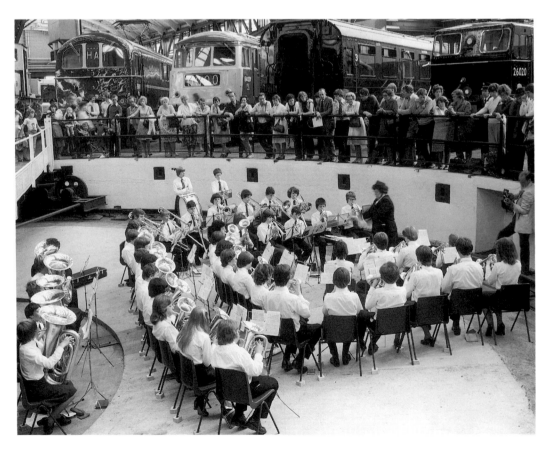

73 Following the precedent set at the opening of the Museum, the turntable pit has been used on a number of occasions for musical events. Here the Salvation Army Youth Brass Band from Sheffield entertains visitors during the summer school holidays. In the background are some of the Museum's more modern exhibits.

(NRM: 1298/79)

74 Besides its attraction as a working exhibit, the reproduction *Rocket* was an important addition to the Collection, appreciated by young visitors. Not only did it fill an important gap in the displays, especially as there were no plans for the original to leave the Science Museum but it was of considerable use to the education staff. In particular it was less sensitive to young hands and feet than the older original locomotives, allowing staff to explain something of the locomotive's significance at close quarters.

(NRM: 1,716/79)

75 In January a 1936 French built Wagons-Lits Sleeping Car No. 3792 was handed over to the Museum by Mr Philip Jefford of the Wagons-Lits Company. The vehicle, representing the international railway scene in Britain, had been used until 1977 on the 'Night Ferry' service between London, Paris and Brussels. It was then purchased by the Museum with considerable help from the Wagons-Lits Company and fully restored at their Ostend Works to as near its original condition as possible.

(NRM: CT RE 75)

76 May 1980 and LMS 4-6-2 No. 46229 *Duchess of Hamilton* sets out from York on its first public working for seventeen years. When withdrawn in 1963 the locomotive was sold to Butlin's Holiday Camp at Minehead. In 1975 it was lent by Butlin's to the Museum and after cleaning and repainting at Swindon Works went on display at York in 1976. Restoration of the *Duchess* to mainline operational order on behalf of the Museum became the first major project for the Friends. With extra support from sponsorship by the fine art publishing company Manuscript Ltd, this fully booked 'Limited Edition' special to Leeds and Harrogate was the successful outcome.

(John Hunt)

77 SR 'Schools' class 4-4-0 No. 925 *Cheltenham* passes Dringhouses yard, York, on a test run after an overhaul at the Museum. The locomotive was still to receive a final coat of paint and livery detail before appearing in steam in the Liverpool and Manchester Railway 150th anniversary celebrations at Rainhill in May 1980. It is seen here with the former Royal Train LNWR service carriage No. 5155 which the Museum used on a number of special steam train workings in the early 1980s.

(NRM: CT 80/08/22)

78 Museum cleaners at work in the yards at Bold Colliery, Lancs, where locomotives and carriages taking part in the Cavalcades to mark the 150th anniversary of the Liverpool and Manchester Railway were stabled.

(NRM: CT RE 78)

79 Museum Midland Railway exhibits in the Liverpool and Manchester 150th anniversary Cavalcade at Rainhill, May 1980. Three cylinder compound 4-4-0 No. 1000 of 1902 hauls a 1914 Dining Car.

(NRM: CT RE 79)

80 The driver's view from the footplate of BR 2-10-0 No. 92220 *Evening Star* during one of the Liverpool and Manchester 150th anniversary Cavalcades. With considerable help from the railway preservation movement the Museum was able to provide over twenty locomotives, carriages and wagons for the Cavalcades.

(John Hunt)

81 The much modified
original *Rocket* of 1829 was
displayed in Liverpool
Museum during the summer
of 1980. As part of the
Liverpool and Manchester
Railway celebrations, *Rocket*
made a very rare excursion
from the Science Museum
back to near the scene of its
original triumph at the Rainhill
Trials in September 1829 and
operations in the early 1830s.

(NRM: CT 80/08/27)

82 During August 1980 the much needed repairs to the roof of the goods depot store afforded this view of the yard outside. At this time the Museum yard was not so large, either in length or width, as today. As a result a number of Museum wagons are seen stored outside the security fence (left of picture). The locomotives, including the *Duchess of Hamilton*, are standing where today there is an ash pit, while the carriages, many sheeted, are standing on the original sidings. These were straightened some years later to provide easier and safer shunting. In the foreground is the Borough Market Junction signal box from London Bridge.

(NRM: 733/80)

83 The dedication of 'Deltic' diesel electric locomotive No. 55002 *King's Own Yorkshire Light Infantry* to the National Railway Museum. In 1980, with the end of service for the 'Deltics' in sight the Museum nominated this locomotive for its collection when eventually withdrawn, under the terms of the 1968 Transport Act. In view of the increasing interest in preserving classic diesel designs, the Friends, with the co-operation of the Eastern Region and the British Railways Board, sponsored the repainting of No. 55002 in near original livery – safety considerations dictated the yellow end panels. The locomotive was also fitted with a small plaque commemorating this event.

(NRM: 1224/80)

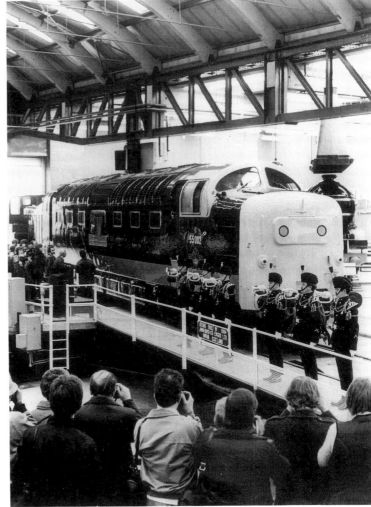

ROCKET.
to
Sacramento · California
from the
National Railway Museum
York · England
Sponsored by
Midland Bank
International

84 The reproduction *Rocket* starts its journey by road and air to the California State Railroad Museum in Sacramento where it took part in the opening ceremonies. Sponsorship was obtained with the help of the Friends and depended very much on banking developments in California at just the right time.

(NRM: 255/81)

85 Museum staff testing a new 7¼in gauge steam locomotive which was built in the Museum workshops for a new miniature railway to demonstrate the operation of steam locomotives for younger visitors. Many smaller children, while fascinated by the sight of full size locomotives in steam, are deterred from approaching too close by its size, noise and heat. This miniature railway proved very popular and very economic to operate. As a result the Museum has been able to provide steam locomotive demonstrations more frequently than with full size machines, which are nevertheless made available for special occasions.

(NRM: 252/81)

86 Sir Arthur Heywood (1849-1916) pioneered work on 15in gauge, or 'minimum gauge', railways to replace the horse and cart for short distance haulage on country estates etc. The Museum's 'Minimum Gauge' exhibition marked the centenary of the first public viewing of his 15in gauge railway. Such railways became the meeting point for railways for transport and railways for pleasure and exhibits represented both categories. In the foreground of this section of the exhibition is the 1909 pioneer Bassett-Lowke steam outline petrol engined locomotive *Blacolvesley* (as LNER No. 1326) and behind is the 4-4-2 steam locomotive *Little Giant* designed by Henry Greenly in 1904.

(NRM: 904/81)

87 A British built locomotive returns from service in China to represent the large and important private railway industry in the National Railway Museum. Following an approach on behalf of the Museum, the Chinese Government kindly donated a 4-8-4 locomotive built in 1935 by the Vulcan Company at Newton-le-Willows. It is seen being unloaded at Gravesend under the watchful eye of its designer, the late Colonel Kenneth Cantlie (centre figure). The minor restoration and repainting necessary before display was funded by the Friends.

(NRM: CT 81/14/14)

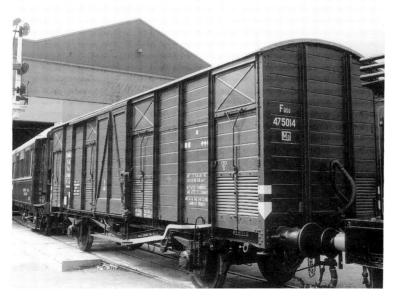

88 In the summer of 1981 French Railways (SNCF) and the French Railway Museum at Mulhouse presented this Paris, Lyon Mediterranée (PLM) train ferry van to the Museum. The vehicle, built in France in 1935 to the more restricted British loading gauge, was mainly used for the rapid through transport of fresh vegetables from the south of France to London via the Dunkirk-Dover train ferry. A similar vehicle was also acquired by the French Railway Museum.

(NRM: 435/81)

89 Interior refurbishment of the Museum goods depot store is here seen in progress. Following replacement of the original slate tiled roof and glass skylights with modern double layer materials to improve thermal insulation the accumulated layers of distemper and white paint were removed to leave a brick finish.

(NRM: 422/81)

90 Repairs to the LNWR Royal Saloon built in 1902 for Queen Alexandra in progress in the Museum goods shed store. To prepare this vehicle for the forthcoming 'Palaces on Wheels' exhibition, it was to be repainted in its former decorated LNWR livery of 'plum and spilt milk'. Repairs included replacing the cracked outer panelling (edge pinned) with panels of 'marine ply' which it was hoped would prove more resistant to movement and drying cracks than the mahogany panels used originally. The repainting was funded by the Friends.

(NRM: CT 81/11/28)

91 General view of the 'Palace on Wheels' exhibition celebrating the wedding of the Prince and Princess of Wales. This photograph from the Balcony Gallery shows 1845 LNWR (GJR) 2-2-2 No. 1868 *Columbine*, suitably decorated, standing on the smaller of the two turntables (now removed) together with the London and Birmingham Railway Royal Saloon built in 1842 for Queen Adelaide. The later and larger Royal Saloons provide an appropriate backdrop.

(NRM: 431/81)

92 The Museum was delighted when their Royal Highnesses, the Prince and Princess of Wales, accepted an invitation to visit the 'Palaces on Wheels' exhibition of Royal Saloons in November 1981. Here the Royal couple are seen leaving one of the 1902 LNWR Royal Saloons. A watchful member of the Museum's warding staff stands by ready to assist if necessary.

(NRM: 755/81)

93 A meal is served in the '55 Club'. During the early 1980s the Museum Pullman cars *Emerald* and *Eagle* were attached, where practical, to the *Duchess of Hamilton* when it was working as 'light engine' or on empty stock. This enabled a special service to be offered to Friends and their guests (a total of 55 passengers, hence '55 Club') with the aim of fund raising. A full meal service (usually breakfast or dinner) was provided by volunteers – Museum staff and Friends. The '55 Club' closed in 1984 when the costs of operational maintenance would have outweighed any benefits.

(NRM: CT 81/35/34)

94 1870 GNR 'Single' 4-2-2 No. 1 in action again on the private Great Central Railway at Loughborough at the end of 1981. Last steamed in 1938 the restoration of this famous locomotive was sponsored for an exhibition in Germany which was cancelled at a late stage. The locomotive has since made demonstration visits to one or two private lines as well as appearing in steam at the Museum on special occasions.

(NRM: CT 81/40/17)

95 In early summer, as part of Maritime Year, the Armement Naval of French Railways (SNCF) presented a special exhibition recalling the three cross channel ships to have carried the name *Côte d'Azur* and all owned by SNCF. The exhibition which provided details of cross channel operations with latest *Côte d'Azur* and other modern ferries, was subsequently shown at the French Railway Museum, Mulhouse.

(NRM: 1481/82)

96 The Museum model railway layout was started from scratch. Staff and visitors alike had long been aware of the need for a working model railway for the Museum's collection of 7mm fine scale models. By 1982 the requirement was considered sufficiently important to justify the necessary resources with the model located in the special exhibition gallery below the Balcony. Museum workshop staff would build the railway, fitting in the work with other projects. Operation was to be automatic with a TV monitor to warn of problems. The model was immediately popular and is still being developed in 1996.

(NRM: 700/82)

97 Filming in the Museum goods depot store with the late Richard Burton and Vanessa Redgrave seen in a railway sequence from 'The Life of Richard Wagner'. In addition to providing locomotives and carriages for filming at York station and elsewhere, the Museum has welcomed the opportunity to provide facilities on site. Despite the disruption and extra work the fees are an important consideration and together with immediate and subsequent publicity, fully justify such projects. For the record the locomotive is GER 2-4-0 No. 490 with the GNR luggage van of 1887. Although the film was made by an Austrian film company the spelling of Munich is in deference to English speaking audiences, the Gothic script being left to convey the sense of place.

(NRM: 681/82)

98 The clock in Queen Victoria's saloon of 1869 is opened ready for winding. Railway history and operation is very much concerned with time keeping and clocks. For many years the Museum made every effort to maintain clocks on exhibition in working order, partly to help conserve the mechanisms and partly to avoid misleading visitors. This included clocks inside carriages, especially the Royal Saloons until evidence of damage to upholstery by moths was found. After an extensive cleaning and deinfestation programme access to most saloons is now strictly limited even for staff.

(NRM: 931/82)

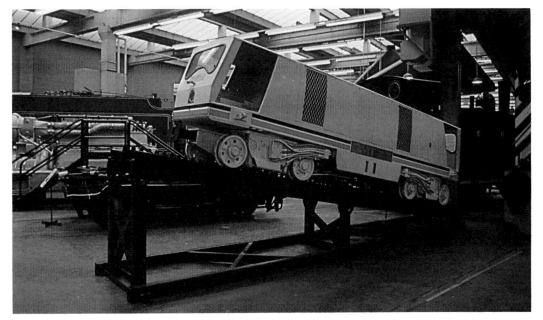

99 A further example of the industrial railway scene was provided by the loan of this modern hydraulic powered rack mine locomotive, complete with a section of special geared track. Destined for eventual use in the Selby Coalfield, then being developed, the display was an interesting, if remote, link with the very origins of the use of vehicles on tracks in the mines of central Europe in the 16th century.

(NRM: CT 82/41/19)

祝・大阪駅リフレッシュ、アクティ大阪誕生
第1回大阪スーパージョイボードオープニング記念春の文化展

機関車のあけぼの

この広告ボードは、文化的エベントスペースとして年2回開放されます。今回はオープニング記念企画として朝日新聞大阪本社のご協力により、"鉄の芸術"ともいわれ根強いファンの多いSLをテーマにとりあげました。ワイドな迫力をごゆっくりご鑑賞ください。

10 DOWNING STREET

I hope that many people, and particularly children, will have the opportunity to see Rocket.

Margaret Thatcher

サッチャー英国首相

主催　（財）日本交通文化協会
後援　日本国有鉄道大阪鉄道管理局　朝日新聞大阪本社

協力　㈱大阪メディア・サービス

資料提供　英国科学博物館

100　In 1983 the Museum was invited by a leading Japanese newspaper to demonstrate the reproduction *Rocket* at an exhibition of railways at Expoland, Osaka. Voluntary help from senior members of the Friends enabled the Museum to accept this opportunity to promote the Museum and a British invention further afield. It was not too far afield however for support from the top – as revealed by this surprising poster on the wall of an Osaka Metro station.

(NRM: CT 83/11/06)

101　Sponsorship for the visit to Osaka came not only from the world of publishing but from famous beverages as well.

(NRM: CT 83/08/18)

102 On its return from Japan the reproduction *Rocket* was requested for the 75th anniversary celebrations of the National Technical Museum, Prague, which had always enjoyed close links with the Science Museum in London. When not in action outside the museum in Prague, *Rocket* made an interesting addition to the very varied collection in the transport gallery.

(NRM: CT 83/48/39)

103 Winter on the Settle-Carlisle line as Midland Railway three cylinder compound 4-4-0 No. 1000 pilots privately owned LMS 'Jubilee' class 4-6-0 No. 5690 Leander away from a water stop at Garsdale, with a southbound 'Cumbrian Mountain Express'. This was to be the last working for the Midland compound which would require a major overhaul before being approved for further main line operations. In due course the Museum took the view that the cost and risks of operating unique historic locomotives such as GNR No. 1, Hardwicke, the Compound and later City of Truro were probably only justified for very special anniversaries.

(NRM: CT 83/03/32)

104 The trailer car from the experimental (gas turbine powered) version of the Advanced Passenger Train (APT-E) displayed in the full 9° tilt position. Although practical and safety considerations prevented the demonstration of the tilt mechanism, the static display, aroused considerable interest. It also focussed attention on the need for an introduction to the engineering of curved railway tracks and the more specific issues of super elevation and cant deficiency for the operation of ordinary trains.

(NRM: CT RE 104)

105 Exhibits from the National Railway Museum and Science Museum helped to foster the Christmas spirit in West Berlin and raise funds for further Museum development. For its special annual Christmas exhibition the famous Berlin department store Ka De We hired a wide range of railway artefacts, including the sectioned reproduction of *Rocket* from South Kensington.

(NRM: CT 83/54/13)

106 This photograph shows the outside of the diesel motive power depot adjoining the Museum (on the right hand side in this picture) and alongside the East Coast Main Line. The depot, together with wheel-drop and small workshop area, was acquired in 1984. To enable the Museum to open its goods shed store as a permanent second exhibition hall it was essential that a further rail connected store, preferably with workshop facilities, was secured in the immediate vicinity. This depot was the ideal solution sharing as it did a party wall with the Museum.

(NRM: 1018/82)

107 The interior of the diesel motive power depot at York in 1984, photographed shortly after acquisition by the Museum, showing the workshop area with the wheel drop in the middle foreground. On the right hand side are the longer straight 'roads', most with inspection pits, already filled with Museum rolling stock much of which is awaiting restoration.

(NRM: 261/84)

108 Although the Museum's education staff had helped school parties and other groups to make good use of the well equipped 80 seat lecture theatre from the outset, they reported an increasing interest in somewhat less formal visit arrangements, especially for younger children. Such an approach was well suited to the open plan nature of the locomotive and carriage displays. These allowed the circulation of other visitors and groups without undue intrusion into informal sessions such as this story telling arranged, in this instance, by the Museum with York Central Library.

(NRM: 419/84)

109 By 1984 the demand for study facilities in the original Reference Library was such that it was decided to extend the library into part of the Art Gallery. The resulting specially furnished reading room, pictured here, provided readers with more space and direct access to selected journals and photographic prints. The Library has enjoyed increasing use and is now known as the Jack Simmons Library in recognition of the Museum's first Honorary Fellow, Professor Jack Simmons, Britain's pre-eminent railway historian.

(NRM: 324/84)

110 Permanent way maintenance machines and equipment, old and new, displayed outside the Museum on the occasion of the 100th anniversary of the Permanent Way Institute. Arranged in co-operation with the Chief Civil Engineer of the Eastern Region, the exhibition included machines from the Museum Collection.

(NRM: CT 84/17/24)

111 To allay concern over safety when nuclear flasks carrying fuel elements are moved by rail, the nuclear industry and British Rail staged a dramatic public demonstration. In this a train crashed into a stationary railway wagon carrying a nuclear flask, the whole event being filmed from several positions. Despite extensive damage to the diesel locomotive and carriages, the nuclear flask suffered only superficial damage. The picture shows the actual flask and wagon used on display outside the Museum which also ran a video of the crash.

(NRM: CT 933/160)

112 The Baroness Thatcher, then Prime Minister, pointing out the locomotive nameplate of a famous predecessor while visiting the Museum with the Chairman of the British Railways Board, the late Sir Robert Reid.

(NRM: BR Y 4/849/6286/12)

113 Although by the end of 1984 consideration was being given to opening the goods shed store to visitors the platforms were still almost completely covered with stored material. It was clear that much more remained to be done in transferring this material, awaiting sorting, listing, photographing and some eventual restoration, elsewhere. Whatever action was taken it was likely that further storage would be required in due course especially if the motive power depot were to be opened to visitors.

(NRM: 30/84)

114 Visitors admiring the interior of former GWR Royal Saloon No. 9006, used by Her Majesty Queen Elizabeth, the Queen Mother, until 1979. The Museum received considerable help from Her Majesty as to how the furniture and other items, including her own china which she donated to the Museum, should be arranged so that the interior was just as it used to be when she travelled in the saloon.

(NRM: 776/84)

115 When Museum locomotives work on the main line they are always accompanied by a Museum representative familiar with that particular locomotive. Here the late John Bellwood, the Museum's Chief Mechanical Engineer, accompanies a York driver on the footplate of *Evening Star* at the head of a special train from York to Hereford.

(NRM: CT 85/15/07)

116 Two visitors obtain a first glimpse of *Mallard* in steam since its preservation. The restoration of *Mallard* to working order in time for the 50th anniversary in 1988 of its world speed record for steam locomotives (126mph/203kph) had been one of the founding objectives of the Friends of the Museum. In September 1985, when the Museum celebrated its 10th anniversary *Mallard* appeared in steam on test, albeit without boiler insulation and streamlined casing.

(Richard Fowler)

117 GNR 'Single' 4-2-2 No. 1 of 1870 was another historic locomotive in steam again for the Museum's 10th anniversary weekend at the end of September.

(NRM: 1357/85)

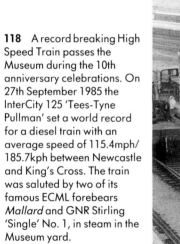

118 A record breaking High Speed Train passes the Museum during the 10th anniversary celebrations. On 27th September 1985 the InterCity 125 'Tees-Tyne Pullman' set a world record for a diesel train with an average speed of 115.4mph/185.7kph between Newcastle and King's Cross. The train was saluted by two of its famous ECML forebears *Mallard* and GNR Stirling 'Single' No. 1, in steam in the Museum yard.

(NRM: 1305/85)

119 During the Museum's anniversary weekend visitors could enjoy rides behind Museum locomotives in the goods shed yard. Here the reproduction *Rocket* with a 1930 reproduction Liverpool and Manchester carriage passes the reproduction GWR broad gauge (7ft 0¼in) locomotive *Iron Duke*. For many it was the first opportunity to see *Iron Duke*, which had been commissioned by the Science Museum on behalf of the National Railway Museum with significant funding from the Friends. The locomotive had been unveiled in Kensington Gardens earlier in the year as one of a number of events to mark the 150th anniversary of the Great Western Railway.

(NRM: 1370/85)

120 As part of the weekend celebrations for the Museum's 10th anniversary visitors were admitted to the goods shed store for the first time. Although many objects remained stored on the platforms visitors were able to view a number of restored carriages and inspect many of the vehicles awaiting restoration. The Museum benefitted from their encouraging response to these ideas for the future use of the building.

(Richard Fowler)

121 A *Mallard* Press Call was held in June 1986. Following the successful completion of steam trials earlier in the year, including a run to Hull and repainting, *Mallard* was ready for its first official public appearance in steam on 18th June outside the Museum.

(NRM: 1032/86)

122 The Museum's LMS electric multiple unit of 1941 (BR class 502) pictured on a special working on the 600/750 volt dc third rail electrified Hoylake line. On long term loan to Steamport, Southport, this unit was restored as a joint project between Steamport and the North West Branch of the Friends with technical assistance from Merseyrail. It attracted considerable interest during the 1980s when it was used on occasional special trains on the Merseyside electric system. The unit is now a static exhibit at Steamport awaiting further maintenance.

(NRM: CT 86/06/20)

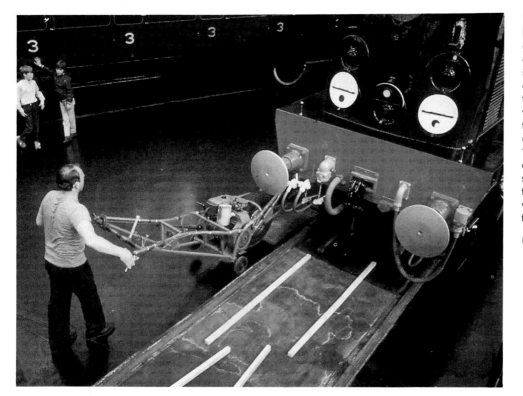

123 Many visitors asked how some locomotives and carriages were moved when access by even a small diesel shunter was obviously very difficult or impossible and traditional methods – levering with crowbars ('pinch bars') – too slow. The answer was to use, as here, a petrol powered 'Locopulsor', originally developed for shunting in small yards. This is driven through the rubber tyred wheel which also serves as the point of leverage.

(NRM: CT RE 123)

124 GWR 4-4-0 No. 3440 *City of Truro* piloting *King George V* with a special train near Dorrington between Shrewsbury and Church Stretton creates the almost quintessential Great Western Railway scene. As another Museum contribution to the proposed 1985 GWR celebrations *City of Truro*, from the GWR Museum Swindon, was restored to main line operational order on the Severn Valley Railway and ran there during 1985.

(John Hunt)

125   In the summer of 1986 *City of Truro*, the first locomotive recognised to have travelled over 100mph (161kph) in 1904, joined *Mallard* at the Museum in York. Here they are seen together receiving attention in the Museum workshops in the former motive power depot, between working special trains on the main line.

(NRM: 1338/86)

126 Another Museum locomotive in action during the summer was *Evening Star*, which went to the North Yorkshire Moors Railway to take part in the 150th anniversary celebrations of the Pickering-Whitby railway. Here *Evening Star* is seen working hard at the head of a train near Green End.

(John Hunt)

127 In a year of considerable high profile activity, often away from York, significant progress was made with important curatorial work 'behind the scenes'. The Museum's large and varied collection of railway uniforms had been sorted, listed and carefully stored, each in its own dust jacket made by a member of staff. These uniforms are often displayed as part of temporary exhibitions associated with special events and anniversaries.

(NRM: 1384/86)

128 French troops photographed boarding a train at Dover after evacuation from Dunkirk in June 1940. This is a picture from the very large Museum archive of railway photographs. It was used in the 'Image of the Train' exhibition in the Museum of Photography, Film and Television at Bradford, as their contribution to the 10th anniversary of the National Railway Museum. The exhibition transferred to York in 1986.

(NRM: 759/67)

129 Much railway equipment, especially that in the public eye, was elaborately decorated and even the simple lettering on this milk tank calls for painstaking preparation and skilful execution. The Museum's sole painter has been fully employed since the opening, usually on the most demanding work, only assisted at times of greatest pressure by contractors or railway works.

(NRM: CT RE 129)

130 In 1987 some major changes were introduced at the entrance to the Museum's main display area. To take account of comments from visitors, particularly school teachers, many of the main exhibits, specially the locomotives, were rearranged so far as practical in a chronological sequence around the turntables. At the same time some of the traditional showcases were replaced with the 'How It All Began' full-size diorama style display. This featured some of the Museum's oldest exhibits and outlined the origins of today's railways.

(NRM: 296/87)

131 Watching Museum staff at work on exhibits or displays always provides interest for visitors. Here a curator is working with the Museum design team to assemble revised showcase displays using some of the Museum's fine collection of engineering locomotive models. The aim is to use the models to show how locomotive design evolved and why, as distinct from a more traditional presentation of the model on its own.

(NRM: CT 87/08/06)

132 The late Terence Cuneo made preliminary sketches at the Museum for a new picture of *Mallard* breaking the world speed record for steam locomotives in 1938, to mark the 50th anniversary of the event. Limited edition prints of the picture were published in 1988, in conjunction with the Friends, as a fund raising exercise.

(NRM: CT 933/172)

133 The small team of Museum cleaners have always kept the exhibits, large and small, routine or glamorous, in splendid condition. Here the special copper pipework on *Evening Star* is immaculate.

(NRM: 21/86)

134 Mechanical signal frames, of many different types had been stored close together in the goods shed store outbuilding for some years. Although this building was not available to the Museum until the mid-1980s it has since enabled better progress to be made in clearing S&T items from the goods shed. Nevertheless, as can be seen from this picture the continued overall shortage of storage space leads to the crowding of objects which in turn limits access for study or restoration of individual items.

(NRM: 277/88)

135 The railways were one of the earliest users of pictorial posters to promote business. By the 1920s they regarded posters as sufficiently important to employ well established artists to provide the original artwork for posters. This one, of the Wye Valley, published by the GWR, is by Frank Newbould. The Museum has built up one of the largest collections in the world of railway posters of Britain, as well as taking over, from the British Railways Board, many examples of the original artwork.

(NRM: CP Inv. 78/38/394)

136 Exhibitions of railway posters from the Museum Collection, on various themes, have always been welcomed by visitors. This one, arranged on the covered smaller turntable in the Main Hall of the Museum, is presented on robust frames which were used when it toured a number of European Railway Museums. It also shows what can be achieved with free standing displays of pictorial material. It was recognition of this that allowed the Museum to convert two galleries for the model railway and the Jack Simmons Library.

(NRM: Neg. 424/87)

137 With the Museum workshops well established in the former motive power depot it was possible to arrange for visitors to look round on certain occasions. Here they inspect progress on the major overhaul of the *Duchess of Hamilton*. The enthusiastic response to this facility has led to the hope that a viewing platform will be provided in any future development of the depot building.

(NRM: 387/88)

138 When the Woking Homes for orphans of railway families closed in 1988 some material relating to its history was acquired by the Museum. It was not possible however to justify the work which would be involved in transferring this elaborate London & South Western Railway design, piece by piece, to York. Instead a photographic record had to suffice.

(NRM: 442/88)

139 BR class 40 English Electric Type 4 diesel-electric locomotive No. D200 poses alongside *Evening Star* in the Museum yard after being handed over by British Rail on completion of its last journey. When the Museum originally considered its modern traction collecting policy D200 was declined on the basis of only having room for a limited number of diesel-electric locomotives. When D200 was finally withdrawn, having been overhauled and repainted in its original livery for use on special trains, the Museum reconsidered its earlier decision and accepted the locomotive. This was because with more yard space it would be able to demonstrate D200 as well as recognising its historical significance.

(NRM: 962/88)

140 3rd July 1988 and *Mallard* heads an InterCity special from Doncaster to Scarborough, run to celebrate the exact 50th anniversary of the world speed record for steam locomotives. The train had been worked from London to Doncaster, where *Mallard* was built in 1938, by a new class 91 25kV electric locomotive. *Mallard* worked the special back to York before going on display in the Museum, while the special returned south behind the electric locomotive.

(NRM: RE 140)

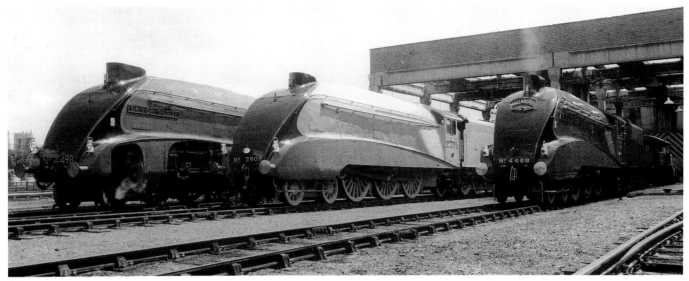

141 After the special *Mallard 88* train on 3rd July 1988, celebrations continued the following day at the Museum where three streamlined A4 class 4-6-2 locomotives could be seen. In a scene reminiscent of LNER publicity pictures they are, from left to right, No. 4498 *Sir Nigel Gresley* (in steam), No. 2509 *Silver Link* (actually No. 60019 *Bittern* repainted in the original two tone silver grey livery for the occasion) and *Mallard*.

(NRM: 239/88)

142 After the July celebrations *Mallard* was thoroughly inspected, including an examination on the wheel-drop in the Museum workshops, before working further *Mallard 88* specials on the main line. These specials, organised by the Friends in conjunction with British Rail and the Steam Locomotive Operators Association (SLOA) were sold out and very profitable.

(NRM: 948/88)

143 A *Mallard 88* special heads south out of York station and underneath Holgate Bridge on its way to Leeds and the Settle-Carlisle line.

(John Hunt)

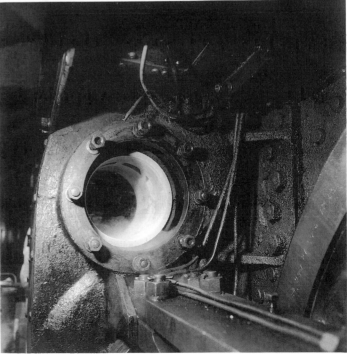

144 With *Mallard* covering an extensive programme of main line specials, the opportunity was taken to carry out minor repairs on LNER 2-6-2 No. 4771 *Green Arrow*. This included shrink fitting a liner, using liquid air, into the valve chest of the left hand side outside cylinder.

(NRM: 1233/91)

145 Narrow gauge (1ft 11½in) double Fairlie 0-4-4-0T locomotive *Livingston Thompson* of 1886 arrives at the Museum from the Festiniog Railway in North Wales. With very few narrow gauge exhibits in the National Collection the Museum welcomed the offer of a long term loan of this unusual locomotive which has one firebox serving two boilers, each with its own set of cylinders.

(NRM: 315/90)

146 The interior of the smokebox of the *Duchess of Hamilton,* showing the front tube plate and superheater flue tubes. Having worked special trains on the main line from 1980 until 1985 the locomotive received a comprehensive overhaul in the Museum workshops between 1986 and 1990. This included major repairs (some off site) to boiler, firebox, cylinders, wheel sets and bearings, lowering the cab (to provide improved clearance under electric wires) and a new tender tank with increased water capacity. The project was organised and funded by the Friends who arranged sponsorship and many various fund raising schemes.

(NRM: CT 936/562)

147 By 1989 although many objects had been cleared from the platforms of the goods shed store, many remained and would have to be stored elsewhere before the building could be opened to visitors. Early in the year a date for this opening was settled by a report condemning the roof of the main Museum building as unsafe from April 1990, due to excessive corrosion in the reinforced concrete roof beams. Rather than close the Museum completely while the roof was repaired or replaced, it was decided to make the goods shed store the Museum from March 1990.

(NRM: 274/89)

148 To meet the various storage requirements arising from the need to replace the Museum roof, suitable storage near the Museum was urgently required. A number of possible buildings had already been considered as part of the long term development of the Museum but rejected. Fortunately a local rail connected former engineering works became available in 1989 and provided a solution. Although the buildings, seen here, required much attention, plans could now be made for the overall Museum programme for the next few years.

(NRM: 1029/89)

149 Operations in 1989 included the appearance of *City of Truro* in a cavalcade of locomotives from all over Europe at Utrecht, as part of the 150th anniversary celebrations of railways in Holland. Here Museum staff, engineering and administrative, male and female, work together on the footplate of the famous locomotive as it passes by the spectators.

(Jane Elliott)

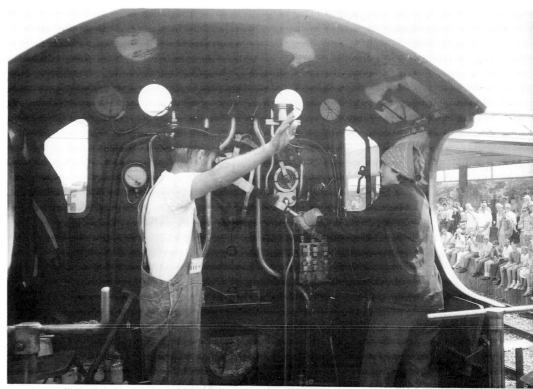

150 For many years the decked smaller turntable had been used not only for exhibitions but for evening functions. One of the last and largest was a dinner in September 1989 for the Museums Association as part of their 100th anniversary celebrations.

(NRM: 1102/89)

151 The operation of the Museum in the goods shed store was known as the 'Great Railway Show' to convey the essentially temporary nature of all the arrangements. As this picture shows however this was not apparent from the actual displays. The overall theme was 'Travel by Train' and dealt more with the social and economic aspects of railways than with technical matters. This approach was welcomed by visitors, many of whom were less familiar with steam locomotives and perhaps railways as a whole than visitors in 1975.

(NRM: 307/90)

152 The Museum 'Brief Encounter' restaurant on the centre platform of the 'Great Railway Show' has proved very popular. Interestingly this bears out the findings of a marketing survey carried out at the planning stage of the exhibition. This revealed that the opportunity for refreshments alongside exhibits, as distinct from eating in a separate area, was rated as highly as any of the proposals for new or revised exhibitions.

(NRM: 303/90)

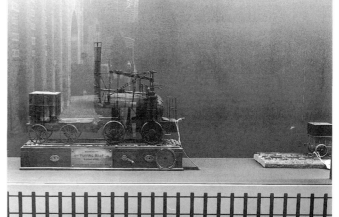

Experimental railway steam locomotive ran on the Penydarren Tramway in South Wales. Designed by Richard Trevithick, this locomotive hauled 10 tons for 9 miles with a top speed of 5 miles per hour.

First commercial use of steam locomotives on the Middleton Colliery Railway in Leeds. The locomotives, built by the Leeds engineers Murray and Blenkinsop, used a form of rack-and-pinion with a cogged driving wheel engaging a toothed rail.

153 As an introductory exhibition to the 'Travel by Train' section of the 'Great Railway Show' a wide range of smaller railway objects were displayed in historical sequence. Prime objects were labelled with the date represented, together with brief details, set against contemporary national and international events.

(NRM: 1050/91)

1804
Napoleon proclaimed Emperor of France

1812
Napoleon retreats from Moscow
Main streets of London lit by gas

154 An innovation in the 'Great Railway Show' was a gallery named 'Magician's Road' (a 19th century description of the railway) set aside for interactive exhibits of various kinds, primarily for use by school parties and families with children. Here children get to grips with signal levers in an original Highland Railway frame, after a brief introduction to the equipment by a member of Museum staff who also keeps watch to see that no one comes to any harm.

(NRM: 74/90)

155 A school party explores the compartments and side corridor of the third class teak panelled East Coast Joint Stock carriage of 1898. With carriages alongside platforms in the 'Great Railway Show' it was possible, at last, to arrange for supervised access to selected carriages.

(NRM: 431/90)

156 *Evening Star* and the prototype HST power car are seen in the 'National Railway Museum on Tour' exhibition in part of the former GWR Works at Swindon. While a much higher roof, to a completely new design was built in the Main Hall of the Museum at York, all exhibits had to be removed. There was however only room for a small number of them at York, either on exhibition in the 'Great Railway Show' or in store. Fortunately with support from Tarmac Swindon Ltd, Thamesdown Borough Council, the British Railways Board and many others including the Friends, it was possible to exhibit the displaced locomotives and carriages at Swindon.

(NRM: 461/90)

157 The written material for the displays in both the 'Great Railway Show' and 'NRM on Tour' was prepared and edited to provide a concise overview of each subject rather than the more detailed statements often previously provided. This approach recognised that visitors were looking for an introduction to the different areas of railway history and engineering to help put the exhibits in context.

(NRM: 465/90)

158 'Working in the Works' was a selection of Museum archive photographs in the 'NRM on Tour' exhibition which showed scenes from life in Swindon Works over many years. Not surprisingly there pictures attracted considerable interest from local visitors and suggested the possibility of a book devoted to this large collection when it has been fully catalogued.

(NRM: 472/90)

159 The original Museum building at York with the roof completely removed. The smaller turntable has also been removed and the pit filled although at this stage traces of the pit and the lines which radiated from it can still be seen. The turntable was removed so that some of the lines, or 'roads', from the larger turntable, just discernable at the far end of the building, could be extended. This would allow, in future, the display of locomotives coupled to carriages or multiple units.

(NRM: 573/90)

160 Staff from the Eastern Region Civil Engineer's York Track Welding School demonstrating their skills in the Museum's goods shed yard. During the summer a number of special events and demonstrations were arranged for the 'Great Railway Show' in addition to the usual miniature railway operations and yard trips behind Museum locomotives.

(NRM: CT RE 160)

161 The imposing statue of George Stephenson being transferred, together with its plinth, from a position on the floor of the Museum to a loftier perch in a niche in one of the two end buttresses supporting the centre girders for the new roof. The statue, by E.H. Bailey, had originally graced the Great Hall at the old Euston station.

(NRM: 1028/91)

162 The then Minister for the Arts, the Rt. Hon. Tim Renton MP, at the controls of the reproduction *Rocket* during his tour of the 'Great Railway Show' in July. The Minister also saw the extensive £5.6 million re-roofing and reconstruction project in the Great Hall (formerly the Main Hall) which had received special funding from the Office of Arts and Libraries. His visit came shortly after the presentation of the Museum of the Year Award for the 'Great Railway Show' and the announcement that the re-roofed Great Hall would re-open in the Spring of 1992.

(NRM: 407/91)

163 A special InterCity 125 train carrying Her Majesty Queen Elizabeth II to Edinburgh, passing the Museum on 28th June. Arrangements were made by the Museum to salute this special Royal Train, marking the completion of the East Coast electrification, as it passed by. *Gladstone*, with its royal decorations and two of the LNWR Royal coaches were displayed outside the Museum together with 'Deltic' *King's Own Yorkshire Light Infantry*. The latter exchanged horn greetings with the electric locomotive on the Royal Train and a cheering party of school children were rewarded with a wave from the Queen.

(NRM: 314/91)

164 Although there was only room for relatively few of the Museum's extensive collection of fine scale models in the 'Great Railway Show', the 'Model of the Month' display helped to redress the balance. In this example, 7mm scale models of typical Highland Railway trains are supported with appropriate small artefacts from silver plated tableware to ticket clippers.

(NRM: 333/91)

165 Final preparations taking place for the re-opening of the Great Hall in April 1992. After years of lying derelict in the goods shed yard, the NER footbridge from Percy Main station on Tyneside is reassembled under the new roof by the Museum's engineering staff.

(NRM: 113/92)

166 The view across the Great Hall under the new roof as seen from the Balcony Gallery. The higher roof creates a sense of greater space and the large exhibits, here already cleaned and polished under the dust sheets ready for the re-opening, will be seen to full advantage without the distraction of the roof supports of the old Main Hall. On the turntable a new exhibit, GWR 4-6-0 No. 4003 *Lode Star*, has just arrived from the GWR Museum, Swindon.

(NRM: 169/92)

167 The Weatherhill winding engine receives last minute attention from one of the Museum cleaners. This engine was one of the few exhibits not to have been moved away while the roof work was carried out. Instead it was completely protected and may now be seen from both inside and outside the Museum.

(NRM: 166/92)

168 The new National Railway Museum was officially opened on 16th April by HRH The Duke of Kent. During his visit he made a short return journey on the Museum's lines in the cab of No. 46229 *Duchess of Hamilton.*

(NRM: 1040/92)

169 By 1992 the 'Please Touch' evenings at the Museum for handicapped groups had become a regular summer event. These visits originated some years ago when staff, realising the difficulties such groups encountered alongside other visitors, volunteered to look after handicapped groups during an evening visit. On such a visit group members could be encouraged to touch and handle exhibits and selected objects were made available specially for them. Individual help is provided for blind visitors and here one, accompanied by his guide dog, feels his way around a locomotive footplate.

(NRM: CT 934/154)

170 Large posters for the new National Railway Museum were displayed alongside the main line just south of York station. Considerable efforts were made to promote the features and attractions of the new Museum. These included enhanced marketing and in conjunction with the Science Museum, the use of a national advertising agency who devised an amusing range of posters including the two seen here.

(NRM: CT 92/16a/18)

171   The new Great Hall by night.   *(NRM: CT 933/037)*

172 At busy weekends and during the school holidays, the Platform 4 Theatre Company have for several years entertained visitors with their lively dramatisations of various aspects of railway life. Here they re-enact the 'Battle of the Gauges', or Stephenson versus Brunel, for visitors watching from standard or broad gauge trains headed by the reproductions of *Rocket* and *Iron Duke*.

(NRM: CT 933/375)

173 Preserved Bo-Bo class 71 electric locomotive No. E5001 pilots class 73 No. 73132 past Totton near Southampton on 12th September, with a Waterloo to Bournemouth charter service. This was the first passenger train on British Rail to be worked by a 'non-steam' preserved locomotive. The class 71 locomotive, from the National Collection, had been returned to full main line condition at the Chart Leacon Depot by arrangement with Network South East.

(Colin J. Marsden)

174 The re-arranged track layout in the Great Hall lends itself more readily to technical demonstrations as well as visits by longer rail vehicles or multiple units. In this instance a demonstration of special private road/rail equipment is taking place.

(NRM: CT 933/467)

175 To attract more visitors during the quieter winter months the Museum's marketing department have explored a number of special evening or weekend events. Not only do such activities encourage more visitors but they provide valuable publicity for the Museum. In November a special 'Antiques Roadshow' for children and young people, called 'The Next Generation' was held in the South Hall and proved a great success. When shown on television at Christmas it is estimated that it attracted an audience of 11.6 million.

(NRM: CT 933/477)

176 GNR 0-6-0ST No. 1247 stands in the undercover workshop yard of the Great Hall where working Museum locomotives or visiting locomotives may be viewed between main line duties. No. 1247, the first privately owned locomotive to work a special train on British Railways in 1959, was donated to the Museum by a member of the Friends after working on a number of private railways. It is seen carrying an American locomotive bell which had just been presented in recognition of its visit to Railfair '91 at the California State Railroad Museum, Sacramento.

(NRM: CT 92/14/25)

177 The proprietary model railway in 'Magician's Road', the Museum's interactive gallery, is designed to be operated by young visitors with help from staff, parents and teachers. Not surprisingly it is rarely out of use and after minor modifications and with the support of the Museum's workshops, has proved remarkably robust.

(NRM: CT 933/912)

178 The 'catwalk' comes to the National Railway Museum. The Museum has been hired to provide a backdrop for a number of television programmes. Since railways and railway stations have often been used in the past as settings for fashion photographs, it is not perhaps surprising that it should host an edition of the 'Clothes Show' in the South Hall.

(NRM: CT 933/551)

179 A view on the revised Balcony Gallery which re-opened in April. When the 'new' National Railway Museum, centred around the Great Hall, was officially opened in April 1992, the Balcony Gallery, along one side of the Great Hall, remained closed. It had been decided to redesign it completely and this required another twelve month's work. It now features a number of the showcase displays previously located around the walls of the Great Hall, completely new displays for the various collections of smaller artefacts, an improved audio visual theatre and a section set aside for special exhibitions of primarily pictorial material such as prints, paintings, posters and photographs.

(NRM: CT 935/237)

180 Restoration to working order (as LMS No. 9395) of LNWR 'Super D' class 0-8-0 No. 485, in progress, supported by private sponsorship. The locomotive which had only recently arrived in York after static display at several sites in the Midlands, required major repairs to the boiler, cylinders, motion, wheel sets and tender tank.

(NRM: CT RE 180)

181 With most of the work on the major exhibitions complete by the middle of 1993, curatorial staff were able to turn their attention once again to the care of stored objects, archival material and many other tasks 'behind the scenes'. Such work includes continuing to sort, conserve, photograph and catalogue the Museum collection of railway company crests . . .

(NRM: CT 936/305)

182 . . . and locomotive nameplates.

(NRM: CT RE 182)

183 The visitor information point in the South Hall is located in a LNER 'passimeter' ticket office, from Winchmore Hill in north London. As part of the programme to improve facilities for visitors, this information point was introduced in the 'Great Railway Show'. Its success led to information points for both Halls in the new Museum, manned by volunteers from the Friends.

(NRM: CT RE 183)

185 The English Electric Co-Co diesel electric 'Deltic' prototype locomotive is unloaded at the Carriage Works, York, on its way to the National Railway Museum from the Science Museum. Moved from South Kensington as part of their long term development plan, the prototype was displayed together with the production locomotive No. 550002 *King's Own Yorkshire Light Infantry*, before the latter moved on loan to the Stephenson Railway Museum, Tyne and Wear.

(NRM: CT 93/20/19)

◄ **184** The 1895 oil painting 'Coming South–Perth Station' by George Earl (1824-1908) was bought in 1990 at auction by the National Museum of Science and Industry together with 'Going North–King's Cross Station', the other painting of the pair. Exhibited initially at the Science Museum while building work at York was completed, they are now displayed at the entrance to the South Hall. The two pictures capture the spirit of the railway age at the height of its prosperity and provide a fitting introduction to the South Hall exhibitions.

(NRM: CT RE 184)

186 The new General Motors built National Power class 59 diesel-electric locomotive No. 59 201 was named *Vale of York* at the Museum on 3rd March before moving on to Derby for type testing a few days later. The American style warning bell, fitted above the cab windows, is not allowed to be used in service.

(Gavin Morrison)

187 Two 70 ton cranes were hired to lift the *Duchess of Hamilton* outside the Museum on 26th July, so that the re-tyred driving wheels could be put back into the frames. These and other repairs which have been carried out on the *Duchess* over the past year, were again financed by the Friends.

(NRM: CT 941/242)

188 The LNER Commemorative Wedgwood plates, featuring cathedrals in cities served by the Company and seen here with other commemorative porcelain, were displayed again as part of an exhibition of cathedral posters. Produced in the 1930s these plates are today very much collectors' items, having a wider appeal than their railway background . . .

(NRM: 90/86)

189 . . . as the origin of their shape, revealed on the reverse side, indicates.

(NRM: 1494/87)

190 A GWR signal gantry from Northolt and diesel locomotive bogies demonstrating two types of automatic signal cab warning systems, enjoy prominent positions in the centre of the Great Hall. The greater size of the new Museum has enabled more space to be devoted to the important subject of signalling including special working exhibits. The extra height of the new roof has allowed the more effective display of signals, especially the gantry.

(NRM: CT 932/968)

191 Below the Library work continues on the sorting, conservation and cataloguing of the collection of mechanical engineering drawings. Although the shelves of drawings may look very much as they did some years ago, considerable progress has been made. It remains to be seen how much the drawing collection will benefit in future from the various computer based cataloguing systems the Museum is currently investigating.

(NRM: CT 933/105)

192 The imposing segment of the Channel Tunnel, incorporated in the Great Hall from 1992, was later joined by a special comprehensive exhibition explaining in general terms how the Tunnel was built. The exhibition, 'The Whole Story', includes many diagrams as well as 'hands on' features and has proved of particular interest to school parties. As a result it has been retained until at least the autumn of 1996.

(NRM: CT 950/394)

193 Another visiting modern locomotive is seen stabled in the Museum in this unusual view from the cab of a locomotive on the Great Hall turntable. This time the visitor is a new dual voltage class 92 electric locomotive No. 92009 *Elgar*, designed to work freight trains to and through the Channel Tunnel. It was itself displayed on the turntable for a conference of the Institute of Mechanical Engineers.

(Gavin Morrison)

194 Important relics still come to light from time to time. This wagon c.1850, from the Stratford and Moreton Tramway was offered to the Museum last year and is now on display in the Great Hall. It is probably the earliest surviving private-owner wagon for use on a public railway. It is in very good condition for its age – even the original lettering survives.

(NRM: CT 941/615)

195 The 1897 Lynton and Barnstaple Railway bogie carriage in its new garden setting. This reflects how it spent the greater part of its life, from the closure of the railway in 1935 until acquired by the Museum in 1982, as a garden summerhouse at Clannaborough Rectory, Crediton, Devon. The idea for this display arose from the recent decision not to attempt any restoration work but to leave the carriage in the relatively good condition, much of it original, in which it was received from the Rectory.

(NRM: CT RE 195)

196 The scene in November, in a darkened Great Hall, when the NER Percy Main footbridge acted as a proscenium arch above an improvised stage and before a full 55 piece orchestra. This was the setting for 'Doing the Locomotion', an evening of music, inspired by railways, presented by the Music Department of the University of York to mark the launch of the Institute of Railway Studies.

(NRM: CP 95/X1/35)

197 The L&Y 2-4-2T locomotive was the setting for this introduction, with a life-like figure in overalls from the collection, to 'Oh! Mrs Porter', a special exhibition depicting the role of women on the railways. The display covered their work from the earliest waggonways to the present day emphasising their special contribution during two world wars. Visitors were able to try their hand at some of the jobs, such as working signals or making station announcements, which the ladies did so well.

(NRM: CP 95/W/07)

198 It is a measure of the expanding scope of the Museum that for some years it had recognised the growing role of railways in children's literature. The Museum had welcomed the Reverend Awdry, creator of the 'Thomas the Tank Engine' stories and his son Christopher, the present author, on a number of occasions including the launch of 'Thomas and the Great Railway Show' in 1991. The Museum was therefore pleased to host a wide-ranging exhibition of Thomas books, toys and other products to celebrate the 50th anniversary of the first Thomas story.

(NRM: CP 95/U/30)

199 The Lancashire and Yorkshire Railway's signalling school gauge 'O' model layout has now been acquired. The Museum had for sometime expressed an interest in this layout, typical of many that had at one time been used to train railway staff. In the aftermath of the Clapham Junction accident in 1988 its disposal was postponed for several years. It is now in store at York and there are plans to re-erect it in the proposed new Interactive Centre where it will enhance interest in working models and signalling.

(NRM: CT RE199)

200 An informative contribution to the Museum's Science Week in March was this demonstration of the fundamentals of the civil engineering involved in bridge building by a team comprising members of the Education and Engineering staff.

(NRM: CT RE 200)

201 For some years the Friends have represented the Museum and themselves at a variety of selected railway and local activities where it was thought that joint promotion could be beneficial. The South of England Group of the Friends travelled to a number of events in their area and found it helpful to use their own portable stand. After sharing this with the York team on a number of occasions, the latter invested in their own equipment. This was first used on a weekend in February at Bury station on the East Lancashire Railway during a working visit by the *Duchess of Hamilton*.

(NRM: CP 96/04/12)

202 The newly appointed Curator of the Photogrpahic Collections carefully examines some of the largest glass negatives in his care. Together with his assistant, also a new appointment, he will be working to make the Museum's large collection of black and white photographs more readily accessible. More storage, environmentally controlled, has recently been provided and progress is now being made with sorting and cataloguing the negatives using a computer. A small team of volunteers from the Friends has just started to help the curatorial team to replace the potentially damaging old negative packaging.

(NRM: CT 960/088)

203 Hats! – a display of railway and travel hats for the Easter Bonnet period. As part of the latest Museum policy to provide a vigorous and varied programme of events throughout the year, a series of smaller special exhibitions, some slightly shorter in duration than previously, has been arranged for 1996. Other exhibitions of this kind feature posters, photographs and new acquisitions.

(NRM: CT 960/053)

204 As part of the continuous Museum improvement programme much of the equipment stored in the South Hall yard since the early 1980s was moved away earlier this year, mainly to other storage in York. The space created has been used to build a family adventure playground and picnic site, bordering the new route of the 7¼in gauge miniature railway. The design for the area was provided by students as part of their HNC garden design course and with local sponsorship and donations this new feature was realised. The Friends Tuesday Night Volunteers built the miniature railway.

(NRM: CT RE 204)

205 The Museum's Interactive Gallery, opened in 1990, has as hoped proved an attraction for younger visitors. The Gallery is always evolving – some displays have been withdrawn as unreliable or unhelpful, while others have been improved. During the past two years completely new relatively self-contained purpose built interactive displays have been introduced. These provide an introduction to some of the fundamental concepts of railways such as wheels on tracks, adhesion, gradients and automatic brakes. Visitor reactions to these exhibits are being monitored and evaluated. The findings will help to provide the basis, along with many of the proven favourites, for more completely new displays in the new Interactive Centre now being planned.

(NRM: CP 96/02/07)

206   Probably the most significant acquisition so far in 1996 has been the Gooch Centrepiece. Made of silver in 1872 it stands thirty two inches high. A striking object with historical detail, it reveals much about Sir Daniel Gooch (1816-1899), who had it made from monies awarded for his work for the Great Western Railway. Today however it has the added interest of being the first object acquired through the Railway Heritage Committee which now ensures the preservation of important railway artefacts for the nation.

(NRM: CT RE206)

207 The traditional fascination of railways continues with school children of today admiring the 1934 sectioned reproduction of the 1829 *Rocket*.

(NRM: CT RE 207)

208 From *Rocket* to 'Eurostar', before long Regional versions of the elegant and successful 'Eurostar' train will be passing the Museum daily with the direct through service between Edinburgh and Paris via the Channel Tunnel. Their route lies along the ECML and then to the west of London before joining the path of the main 'Eurostar' service to and from Waterloo International at Factory Junction, Clapham. Here a 'Eurostar' train from Waterloo crosses the West of England main line and approaches Factory Junction, en route to the Tunnel and Europe.

(Milepost 92¹/₂)

209 Until the arrival of the Regional 'Eurostar' trains, visitors are able to gain an impression of trains to come from the Museum 'Eurostar' mock-up.

(NRM: CT RE 209)

Bibliography

THE FOLLOWING publications provide further information about the origins, objects, collections and work of the National Railway Museum.

Various editions of guides to the Railway Museum, York and the Museum of British Transport, Clapham, London (1927-1972).

Renaissance from Rust – *King George V* (1968-1973). G. Wood. 6000 Locomotive Association, Hereford 1973.

Britain's Railway Museums. P. Williams. Ian Allan Ltd 1974.

Gresley and Stanier – a centenary tribute. J. Bellwood & D. Jenkinson. HMSO 1976. 2nd edition 1986.

Selections 1-6 – collected reproductions of the labels for some of the more important objects. NRM 1976.

Taking the Train – Railway Travel in Victorian Times. P. Bignell. HMSO 1978.

North London Railway – a pictorial record. Ed. P. Atkins & J. Edgington. HMSO 1979.

Centenary Express – a guide to the NRM Catering Centenary Train. D. Jenkinson. HMSO 1979.

Dandy-Cart to Diesel – the National Railway Museum. J. Simmons. HMSO 1980.

Palaces on Wheels – Royal Carriages at the NRM. D. Jenkinson & G. Townend. HMSO 1981.

Greyhound 120 (T9 class 4-4-0 No. 120). P. Cooper. Urie S15 Preservation Group Publications 1983.

Broad Gauge. L. Day. HMSO 1985.

City of Truro – a locomotive legend. N. Harris. Silver Link Publishing Ltd 1985. 2nd edition 1992.

Image of the Train – a 10th birthday present for the NRM. J. Simmons. NMPFT 1985.

The National Railway Collection. Ed. D. Jenkinson. Collins 1988.

Mallard – the Record Breaker. M. Rutherford. FNRM 1988.

Great Railway Show – a Souvenir Booklet. NRM 1990.

NRM on Tour – Swindon 1990 (a souvenir booklet). NRM 1990.

Duchess of Hamilton – Ultimate in Pacific Power. M. Blakemore & M. Rutherford. NRM 1990.

Happy as a Sand-Boy – early railway posters. B. Cole & R. Durack. HMSO 1990.

1247 – Preservation Pioneer. W. Smith. Silver Link Publishing Ltd 1991.

Making of the Modern World. Ed. N. Cossons. John Murray (Publishers) Ltd/Science Museum 1992.

Railway Posters 1923-1947. B. Cole & R. Durack. Laurence King 1992.

Perspectives on Railway History and Interpretation. Ed. N. Cossons. NRM 1992

Image of the Train – the Victorian Era. J. Simmons. NMPFT 1993.

Right Lines – a Teachers Activity Guide to the NRM. D. Mosley. NRM 1993.

Steam Alive – Locomotives of the National Railway Collection in Steam. I. Smith. FNRM 1993.

York Through the Eyes of the Railways. B. Cole/C. Heap. NRM 1994.

The National Railway Collection – locomotives and rolling stock (illustrated booklet). NRM/FNRM 1995.

Various editions of the Museum Guide. 1975-1994.

The illustrated quarterly Newsletter of the Friends of the National Railway Museum, circulated to members, contains regular features about Museum acquisitions, exhibitions, locomotive operations and other developments.

All these publications may be consulted by appointment in the Reading Room of the Jack Simmons Library and Archive of the National Railway Museum. For further information or to book an appointment, please telephone 01904 621261.

Acknowledgements

COMPILING THIS COLLECTION of photographs and the captions would not have been possible without the willing assistance of many people. I am grateful to all who have helped in any way and although it is not possible to mention all concerned, I particularly appreciate the support and encouragement received from:

The Friends, especially their Chairman Professor J. Allan Patmore CBE, Ian Johnson (Chairman, FNRM Enterprises Ltd), John Gilks, William Greenwood, David Humphreys, Brian Knowlman and Dr Arthur Lowe.

The Museum, where many staff, past and present, helped in many ways; in particular:

Andrew Scott, Head of the Museum for his interest and ideas as well as approving overall Museum support.

Christine Heap, Curator, Special Projects, for her constructive editorial comment as well as organising, with patience and understanding all the very necessary liaison between Museum, Friends, Publisher and Compiler.

Philip Atkins and Lynne Thurston in the Library together with Ed Bartholomew, Curator of Photographic Collections.

and Chris Hogg, Lynn Patrick and John Perkins in the Photographic Studio.

A number of leading railway photographers who kindly provided pictures which are credited individually.

The publishing team of David Joy and designer Barry C. Lane.

John Coiley